Ocean Currents

poems by

Hannah Rousselot

Finishing Line Press
Georgetown, Kentucky

Ocean Currents

Copyright © 2021 by Hannah Rousselot
ISBN 978-1-64662-520-8 First Edition
All rights reserved under International and Pan-American Copyright Conventions. No part of this book may be reproduced in any manner whatsoever without written permission from the publisher, except in the case of brief quotations embodied in critical articles and reviews.

ACKNOWLEDGMENTS

"Vacation," *The McNeese Review,* Volume 56
"Immersed," *Underfoot Poetry,* 07/03/18
"By the Lake," *Broadkill Review,* 06/30/18
"Sleepwalking," *The Wild Word,* Issue 31
"Reserve Battery Power," *Alt Minds Literary Magazine,* Issue 1
"Modern Witch," *Dirty Girls Magazine,* Issue 1
"The Dead Sea is the Lowest Place on Earth," *The Blue Nib,* 08/09/19
"Dead End," *Dual Coast Magazine*
"i am learning to be alone, slowly," *Kissing Dynamite,* Serenity Zine
"Acrobat," *Les Femmes Folles*
"Hollow," *Underfoot Poetry,* 07/03/18
"is it too tender to kiss?" *Boudin* (The McNeese Review online)
"Flipside," *Short Edition*

Publisher: Leah Huete de Maines
Editor: Christen Kincaid
Cover Art: Hannah Rousselot
Author Photo: Hannah Rousselot
Cover Design: Elizabeth Maines McCleavy

Order online: www.finishinglinepress.com
also available on amazon.com

Author inquiries and mail orders:
Finishing Line Press
PO Box 1626
Georgetown, Kentucky 40324
USA

Table of Contents

Vacation	1
Leather Gloves	2
Reserve Battery Power	4
pulled apart	5
By the Lake	6
Hollow	7
how to tell if you're depressed	8
Sleepwalking	9
Appeal	10
Synthesis	11
Feast	12
Reminder	13
Dead End	14
by sin I mean insanity	15
Good Little Girls	16
messages from the silent	17
word (verb)	18
Modern Witch	19
Immersed	20
i want a little honey	21
Guidance	22
is it too tender to kiss?	23
Immediate / Transitory	25
i'm learning to be alone, slowly	26
Acrobat	27
Flipside	29
The Dead Sea Is the Lowest Place of Earth	30

Dedicated to all my therapists

Vacation

What if you could kill yourself,
but like, only for a day? You know,
it could be a super cute date with death.
If you wore that red lipstick and flirted
a little, I'm sure you could escape the long corridors
of your mind for a hot second. Just long enough
for you to catch your breath in adorable hiccups
over a glass of Chardonnay. You could dazzle
him with your smile; maybe he'll even ask you
to stay over. You're *definitely* that kind of girl,
but not with him. You only want one day away.
You get back to your life, zip on your body
like an old dress and press play on time.
Everything is where you left it, huge and fearsome
and vigorous and filled with blood.

Leather Gloves

I often see myself as this:

A huddled little girl clutching
her favorite blanket in her dark closet.
She stuffs her sobs in that blanket,
trying to quiet the crying that slips out when
she sees an open wound unacknowledged,
seeping freely into the concrete we all stepped on.

Then she spirals
        and thinks of parents who die
without ever seeing their children
        and children whose insides die
because their parents couldn't keep their hands off them.

I named them my "world hurts"
because it was too hard to cup both their hurt
and mine within my cold, soft hands.

In college, I tell my friend about my
"world" hurts and she tells me
that I have a superpower.

The sensitivity that makes me shake
and moan and hollow, that made my mother
drop me off at the neighbor's at two am
because I cried too much and she was afraid
of herself—is something to aspire to?

I wonder what kind of superpower
makes my mother's face look like that:
eyebrows connected, mouth as thin
as the image I balance around her.

I wonder what kind of superpower
makes your father tell you that
you can't watch the news and yell that
you have to stop *stop* crying
& how can you be adult with so much
child inside of you?

Desperate, my mother once took me aside & said,
"Here is the secret: you need a leather glove
to cover it all. Use it over & over & over until it
can crack but not break, until it can hold
all that is within you without spilling.
Think of your grandfather on his boat,
think of his thick gloves, think of his gift—
he hasn't talked about his son since he buried him."

My hands are too small for gloves,
but I promised I would try anyway.

Reserve Battery Power

the room could crumple, fold in on itself like a wilted flower—
a man could break down the door with a gun and hurt us—
I could burn my hand getting the saucepan and splash red on the carpet—
the driver could decide not to stop for pedestrians—
(will I forget to breathe if I am asleep?)
the sun could make my eyes smolder and shrivel in my face—
my tears and screams and fight could crumple—
I might be irreparably broken—

(i don't want my body anymore why don't i want my body, what did you do to me, oh what did i do to myself, my breath feels like ice but my blood my blood is *boiling*)

pulled apart

Coming to a theater near you:
a young woman holds a
wine glass and slides the words
"I'm losing my mind" like a
hundred dollar bill. A tear falls
into her food, seasons it perfectly.

Coming to a bathroom next door:
the poet holding the words
"I'm losing my mind" like a
plastic knife. Her favorite
shirt collecting sweat stains;
her sweatpants collecting blood.

Suicide would be as sweet
as a freshly peeled tangerine.
Suicide is choosing when
to slam your own door
so the noise doesn't surprise you.

The glass holding her toothbrush
would look best smashed
into pieces no gold could fix.

The syrup of her own blood
would taste just as good as the food
the protagonist doesn't put in her mouth.

By the Lake

I went outside to smoke a bowl
(because my boyfriend was still sleeping
because the sunrise was magical
because I had no real reason, just desire).

While I was standing out there, my coat wrapped
tight around me and smoke wrapped
loosely around my vision, I saw the geese.

Well, I heard them first—outraged honks
and splashing water and the beating of wings.
Chasing, fighting, they would rise in the air
like deities and fall back into the water
like bullets. Finally getting high, I start to think of

my students, all of whom know what a gun is.

Hollow

Glasses clink and
mouths smile and
jewelry sparkles and
eyes are hungry hawks.

This dress is too tight.
My smile is too tight.
My stomach is too tight.

I wish I could peel off my skin
to stretch it out over the curve of the Earth.
Maybe I would finally be skinny enough.

I wish I could give away pieces of my brain
until the light that shines behind my eyes
no longer reflects me, standing alone in the mirror.

how to tell if you're depressed

food tastes like sandpaper and
your stomach shrinks to the size of a pebble.

everything around you loses a layer of life,
like wallpaper peeling off. you stand still in a twirling

world, watching it spin by and unable to really touch it.
you start to forget what you look like. When you try to conjure

up your face, there's nothing but smooth skin.
you stand in front of the mirror, practicing emotions,

trying to memorize what it looks like to be alive.

Sleepwalking

When all of the circuits and electricity and periphery
of the world are dead, when all that is left is

the cold ice of life coursing through her veins—
that's when her window opens. The fire

that animated her, her family, her existence
has frozen solid, a lump deep in her stomach.

They were right; the world is flat. unmoving. barren.
The knife in her hand will only bear fruit

if she uses it to open her skin.
Life is shallow, most of the time.

It needs a reminder to wake up.

Appeal

The water flow brings not
        salvation but jagged seaglass
that burrows within the callused skin
        of my big toe and stubbornly refuses
to break out until I get out my cheap knife
        and cut around the skin but by then
my fingers are too bloody to get a good grip.
        Still, the waves crash in the cavity
of my swollen head and at least my viscous fingers
        feel so good sliding on cheeks.
I am pushed and pulled relentlessly by the moon
        up and down, a dead body floating and sinking.
I want pity from the sand beneath me
        but it burns my back and provides no solidity.
I yell—*I am trying to become one of you*—
        yet the words are cement and I choke
on the salty spray and besides no one is here but
        my want and my want and
no ocean is big enough for that.

Synthesis

When the world peels around me
the first advice I get is: breathe.

Which I guess if helpful,
if you want to breathe.

I don't want to breathe.
Or exercise, or eat, or drink water.

I just want to lie at the bottom
of a grave. It doesn't have to be mine;

I just need to watch the dirt
slowly melt the horizon out of the sky

until it gets into my marrow,
until all my choices tighten

and there is but one left:
the darkness, within me.

The silence, cradling me.
The blindness, allowing me

me to see myself. My body,
gone. My mind, gone.

Just me, and the soil
that I was buried in.

Feast

It would be delightfully delicious
to rip out my veins from my wrist,
slowly, caringly, so that they come out
in strings I could put in a bowl like spaghetti.
If I am lucky the nervous system
would come too, delicate tissue
that crunches between my teeth
like the kale I'm always told to eat.

What if I sucked the marrow out of my bones,
porous softness on the flesh of my tongue,
so that my bones would be empty and ready
for a different seasoning? Would that be enough—

enough to fix the compulsion residing in my joints?
enough to fix my sad-sick flesh?
enough to make my brain want to live?
enough to *fix me*?

I feast on myself,
hoping to make room for something new.

Reminder

I looked out my car window—not really though; my mind was
full of my empty stomach and rising illness—and I saw a filthy crow
with a strip of red flesh hanging down from its beak. I expected to see
blood dripping down its side, but it was strangely dry. The dead
rat was still at its feet, back arched comically towards
the May sun on that early Tuesday morning. I had
a fleeting thought (*death sure likes to show off*)
before putting my car into drive and thinking
of less unpleasant things. My nausea had
strangely and suddenly dissipated,
as if the sight of something
both so grotesque and so
habitual had driven it
away. By the time
I arrived at work,
I had successfully
forgotten the
entire
filthy
thing.

Dead End

I promised myself that today
I would knock on your door to ask if you love me.

Standing in my underwear, I assess myself
in front of the mirror. I dig my fingernails

into the flesh on my thighs. But then I remember
what my therapist told me, so I pick

at my hangnails instead. I pull at one,
the stringy pain exquisite, and it's only when

the skin rips off and the blood pops
to the surface that I am ready.

I have to take an Uber because my body
is shaking too hard for me to walk.

At your door, my breath escapes me.
A promise to yourself, I think

*is like a promise to no one. No one
waits to hear how this went.*

Tomorrow, I have a good feeling about tomorrow.

by sin I mean insanity

I've never believed in a forked tongue
slithering dry lies into my female ears
to damn all of humanity before it began.

I do believe in carrying a sin that cannot
be forgiven or erased. I've carried it in a cute backpack
that my friends compliment, despite that it
glows under apple trees and is full of plasma.

I lasted fifteen days without smoking.
Well I think it was fifteen days because my
therapist says counting days is counterproductive
the same way picking my belly button and breasts

until they bleed is counterproductive. I am supposed
to turn my addiction away from "when will my next high come"
to "I can do this without being high" and my sobriety from
"how long have i been sober" to "today I choose to be sober"

but honestly being sober feels like you've left the stove
on and burned the cat to ash. Sober makes the backpack
ugly and gross and weeping. Sin drips out of it and now
everyone can see it and it changes their faces into masks

of smiles hiding their constant concern. Is it so much to ask
for no one to worry about me? The sin was not meant for
humanity—it was meant for me, specifically. The sun does
not revolve around the earth; it revolves around me.

Being high is like being in a storm cloud: formless, opaque,
freezing, distant. Clouds have no sin within them;
they were never damned at birth. They are like
succulents: soft to the touch but unyielding unless

you get violent. When I snap them they weep.

Good Little Girls

I tell him I want to pierce my nose
to stain away the obedient air that still hung around me.
It's like an uncomfortable skin, it grates me
to be seen as something so controlled and unblemished.

To stain away the obedient air that still hung around me
I spread my legs and smile politely.
To be seen as something so controlled and unblemished
is false advertisement. Just take a look at me:

I spread my legs and smile politely.
That moan (discharged experly from my throat)
is false advertisement. Just take a look at me:
I open my skin to make sure I still bleed.

That moan (discharged expertly from my throat)
is all you really wanted; proof of your ability.
I open my skin to make sure I still bleed
at the same time that I pee to make sure I don't get a UTI.

Back in bed, he tells me he prefers me innocent.

messages from the silent

Everything has a language that pours
destiny onto my frozen tongue.

The first song that shuffle has chosen
tells me whether I should obsess about
the unseen look my supervisor had
when I called with a vice around my lungs
and had to take another day at home.
That first song is an unambiguous crystal ball.

When I drove my sister to the mall and saw
two dead squirrels on the road, one after another,
it was an omen that I would murder us both
on our way to Barnes and Noble. I turned
the car around, and we both lived to see tomorrow.
Any roadkill is a message that the day
would best be lived inside. The blankets are
always soft and inviting and never, ever

suffocating.

word (verb)

It is so luscious, so excruciating,
so compelling to think what I
can pull apart with my mouth.

When I get really bad, and I mean *really*
bad, like want to suicide bomb my own life
bad, like want to no longer exist bad—

that's when I start seeing the spaces
between things rather than the things
themselves. Between the cracks

of my life there are the threads, the words,
that hold it all together, oh so gingerly.
Words that melt and words that peel;

words that change and words that rebuild.
They are woven promises, golden
compliments, watery complaints,

those words—dull, sharp, tender.
If I pull here, and tug there, I can find
the right words to make you hate

that I ever lived, to implode my life
with my own silver tongue. I can pluck
the words like raspberries, sour and

soft—words to make you pucker and spit
and burn the ground I walk on.
The embers would be another way

to justify my misery. But they are just *words*—
they only become a verb if I don't gulp them
down like medicine before they touch my lips.

They taste even sweeter going down
than coming up. They are an inferno outside,
but inside my throat they become melting ice.

Modern Witch

I'm easily recognizable by my
    tattoos   piercings
    unshaven legs   unwashed hair
    dripping sexy   dripping heavy
    spooling love   spinning addiction

Be careful! Modern Witches like me hold grudges.
You don't want to cross me. I will turn my back
on you and cast you out with the spiders. Your words
will turn to sand crumbling out of your mouth, coating
your tongue with dry specks of dirt. It's what I do;
I'll cast a spell on you without hesitation, make you
always think of me when they play "Toxic" by Britney
Spears, make you buckle with me and quiver without me,
make you eat cobwebs for just the privilege of being near
my supple flesh. Men are like cotton candy; so sweet
in your mouth but gone too quickly. If after I have banished you

you come near my home I will rip you to shreds. I will forsake you,
ruin you, emasculate you. I don't need spells for that; I can just use
my sweet tongue, the one you were fine using (for your own benefit)
just a few days ago. It's easy to break you down, and I will use
my dark broom to sweep the rest of you out the door.

Immersed

The water feels like silk against the goosebumps on my skin.
Most wouldn't swim in a pond in late February

but I have always been a ball of heat. The ice
in the water is a wakeup call, a punishment, a cry for help.

Maybe I shouldn't have left my home without speaking
or looking or feeling first. Maybe if I was a better girlfriend

or daughter or teacher I wouldn't have had to run
so that I can remember that my legs are there.

When I rise out of the pond, water drips down
my skin and sinks into the ground. The Earth is soft

between my toes. Standing there, wet
and grounded, I can feel the rotation of my planet.

i want a little honey

while floating in the sea—
a little sweetness to complement
with the salt drying out my lips

a little honey to pour on my face
while tears flow into the waves
and feed the fish—who knows?

maybe they want a different kind of salt;
one that comes from up above, from
rent and viruses and unemployment

"it's so exotic" they would tell their
fishy friends "and it even has a syrupy
golden hue that blinds me so i swim

without seeing what's in front of me
and that is charmingly dangerous,
it gets the gills moving, the scales shining"

maybe i will feel their little teeth tickle
my toes and my legs and my arms
but who knows if fish even have teeth

and there is no way i could get honey
so far out from the shore the people
look squished from out here but if i stop

floating the fish will surely eat me then.

Guidance

I.
I once heard a story
about a city where there were

no stop signs
no road signs
no speed limit.

This city (which used
to feel far but now is
available to my fingertips)
has very few car accidents.

II.
I teach four year olds how to grow,
how to blossom, how to hold each other
so softly. I teach them to love books,
to ask for help, to stand up for themselves.

Or, I should say, I do not teach them—
I provide the tools they need to live within themselves.

The other day, one asked me how to spell shark
and then told me "I love you." The other day,
two were fighting and a third went up and said
"No thank you. How can we make this better?"

III.
Water never takes a shape
when you force it to.

If left alone, water will form

rivers   lakes   oceans

        bodies.

is it too tender to kiss?

I.
in the past, i always held my wounds out
gaping and red, hoping someone would notice
and want to kiss me better.

many ignored and many tried,
but none could re-knit
my skin, my heart, my brain
with strands from their own body.
i had to do it myself—with blood
dripping down my hands and making
my thread slippery, hard to hold.
making my hands slippery,
hard to kiss.

II.
today, while trying to cut stale bread,
i sliced open the meaty muscle
that makes my thumb move.

i called you six times, crying.
i needed you to kiss and make it better.
you were in a meeting, so i decided to grit
my teeth and go to cvs for advice. (even now,
i can't trust my own perception of my hurt)
the pharmacist told me i didn't need stitches

and i listened to her despite my soaked-red
paper towel. i bought bandaids and went home.
you saw my text and came home right away.
then you saw the blood and smelled the panic
and hugged me and drove me to the hospital.

you waited with me while the doctor used her
needle to sew me back together. she said it
was a good thing i didn't listen to the pharmacist
and i told her the truth; you were the one

who said we had to come here. if it were up
to me, i would have bled through those bandaids
for hours yet. you drove me home and held
my tender hand in yours.

later, much later, we are sitting on the couch.
i go to take something off the table and wince.

you take my hand softly
and ask, "is it too tender to kiss?"

it is strength to heal on your own.
but it is strength, too, to accept a kiss
when you desperately needed one.

Immediate / Transitory

I can taste the velvet flavor
of time. The train will be coming soon.
                I am rooted. I watch
                as the world revolves around me,
                thinking blankly: *it should stop*
                when I am stuck in this sludge.
Here is the real truth:
the train is arriving.
This bench cannot, will not, keep me.
                There is something caught in my brain.
                It tugs at me. It is stitches, still in a wound.
                It is space, still bleeding. It is blood,
                still agitating, frothing, contracting.
Time is tangy, and urgent.
The train is pulling in now, coming closer
to my tree-trunk brain.
                It is seeping now, sweating out of my skin
                yet invisible. If I look too closely at it,
                it will disappear. If I look too closely at it,
                it will appear. If I look too closely at it,
                it will overtake me.
There is no more time.
The train is here, and I have to get on.
I cannot worry at the wound now.
                It retreats resentfully,
                vibrating through my bones.
                It is not gone, but it is no longer *here*
I can gather myself. I can pull myself
out. I need to get on this train.
                It will wait, but not for long.
                It will wait, but only because it's forced.
I get on the train.
Eventually it will reach its stop.

i'm learning to be alone, slowly

it started with a tattoo, a walk,
a breakup. i kept it going in increments—
ten minutes at the coffee shop,
twenty minutes in a cozy clothing store,
fifty minute strolls, eventually a two hour
movie. it's easier if i have a goal in mind
and my therapist said that was okay,
for the beginning, not that i need her permission
she reassured me, even though i totally do.

apparently it's important to be alone
so that i can find the elusive taste of self-love,
so i can weather myself. so i can survive
the waves that churn steadily inside.
they are created by me; but when the current
starts pulling at my legs i can find my
island and my point to my lighthouse;
those are created by me, too. there exists
a shore somewhere here—i'll find it soon.

Acrobat

I can trace the line
that divides my brain into half
with delicate feet and callused toes.

Sometimes, my balance is on point.
There is no fear of falling; I drink
my coffee and write my poetry
and kiss my life full on the lips.

Sometimes, the thread is frayed
and the bottom is a thousand
kilometers away begging, begging
for me to see it from her perspective.

Down there, up is down and sick is healthy
and hurt is good. My reflection whispers to me
(*you can't be trusted with yourself, you need
to control it all, don't let it seep out, I do this
because I love you*) and it feels easy, so delicious
to dive in without looking back, like jumping off
of a waterfall where the bottom is concealed but
the pool I see is a beautiful, deep blue.

I know it is best to stay put, to not give in,
to "be stronger than your illness" and to
"love yourself the right way" but oh those
impulsive decisions are a sweet nectar
salve on my raw brain. She knows just what to say,

that reflection of mine, to make all the therapists
and psychiatrists and friends and lovers sound
like they don't know shit about me or my life.

I used to look her straight in the eyes, encourage
her words, and fall without resistance.

Now, I look her straight in the eyes and call her a bitch.
I've worked too hard on my routine; I will not fall
for her lies. I know the bottom is sharp and I refuse
to impale myself again. It hurts too much, *not in a good way*.

At least for today.

Flipside

If you find my sorrow
        keep it. It has been too long

festering and coagulating
        and self-congratulating.

And I, unbound by it,
        might maybe hopefully finally

reach those floating cities
        perched on colossal turtles

whose shadows we grieve under
        and leave us begging for purchase.

But probably likely doubtlessly
        I will just end up pining for it

the same way the sand longs for
        the tiny creatures leaving their eggshells

that disturb its grainy pattern
        and leave into turbulent and bitter water.

The Dead Sea Is the Lowest Place of Earth

This place holds power.
It's hard to believe, standing here
surrounded by tourists (including me)
and stands selling "Restorative Dead Sea Mud!"

but it's true.

It makes sense, if you think about it,
that the lowest place on Earth would also
have the only surface you can float on;
contradictions are what keep us breathing.

I step into the water. I can feel the salt
tickling my ankles. As I go in further,
my skin starts to sting and remind me
of every recent red cut on my body.

I'm already floating, without realizing.
The sky above me is mirror-blue,
reflecting myself. Here, in this between

place, I think of how the truth
is really as thin as a strand of hair.

Hannah Rousselot (she/her) is a queer French-American poet, writer, and educator. Her poetry has appeared in many publications, including Parentheses Magazine, Kissing Dynamite, The McNeese Review, and The Blue Nib. She has published two long works, Fragments of You (Kelsay Press) and Ocean Currents (Finishing Line Press). She also reviews other poet's works on hannahrousselot.com and is the host of the podcast Poetry Aloud.

You can follow her work on facebook.com/hmrpoetry or @hannahrousselot, or hannahrousselot.com.

www.ingramcontent.com/pod-product-compliance
Lightning Source LLC
LaVergne TN
LVHW041507070426
835507LV00012B/1395